AF598987

BOWHUNTING

BY CLARA MacCARALD

childsworld.com

Published by The Child's World®
800-599-READ • www.childsworld.com

Photography Credits
Photographs ©: Zoran Orcik/Shutterstock Images, cover, 1; iStockphoto, 5, 7; Kanawa Studio/iStockphoto, 9; Neil Podoll/Shutterstock Images, 10; Sanit Fuangnakhon/Shutterstock Images, 11 (top); Jeffrey B. Banke/Shutterstock Images, 11 (middle); Shutterstock Images, 11 (bottom), 13, 15, 19; Kolton Bachman/Shutterstock Images, 16; Angie Selman/Shutterstock Images, 20; Bogdan Denysyuk/Shutterstock Images, 21

ISBN Information
9781503869707 (Reinforced Library Binding)
9781503880979 (Portable Document Format)
9781503882287 (Online Multi-user eBook)
9781503883598 (Electronic Publication)

LCCN 2022951127

Printed in the United States of America

ABOUT THE AUTHOR

Clara MacCarald is a freelance writer with a master's degree in ecology and natural resources. She lives with her family in an off-grid house nestled in the forests of central New York. When not parenting her daughter, she spends her time writing nonfiction books for kids.

Contents

CHAPTER ONE

The Blind

Finn and his mother sit inside their ground blind, watching the deer trail. A blind is a small shelter that hides a hunter. The blind has camouflage walls. Camouflage is a pattern that blends into a background, such as a forest or grassland. Both hunters also wear camouflage. If they stay quiet and still, deer won't notice them. Finn and his mother set up the blind weeks ago. They know deer are often afraid of new objects that appear in the forest. But now the deer have grown used to the blind.

Today Finn and his mom are bowhunting. Finn slips on safety goggles to protect his eyes. He holds a **compound** bow. This type of bow uses special wheels and cables to shoot faster than a **traditional** bow. Finn has been practicing with the bow for weeks. He clips an arrow onto the bowstring.

Suddenly, a buck walks by the blind. A buck is a male deer. Finn raises his bow and draws the bowstring back until it reaches a place that's easy to hold. He holds steady, careful not to aim at anything he doesn't mean to shoot. His mom reminds him to never let go of the bow with the string back. This way, he can avoid injuring himself or others.

Bowhunters must make quick decisions while on the hunt. It can be helpful to practice shooting in different positions, such as standing, sitting, or kneeling.

Finn aims through a device called the sight, which is attached to his bow. The sight looks like a magnifying glass with pins. Each pin is set for aiming from a different distance. Finn's goal is to hit the deer's chest, where the heart and lungs are. Shooting the correct place on the animal will mean a clean kill. This means the shot will kill the animal quickly so that it suffers less.

Finn releases the arrow. It flies from his bow straight into the buck's chest. The buck falls to the ground. Finn grins. He's successfully hunted his first deer!

Bowhunting has a long history. Arrow points found in South Africa date back to 61,000 years ago. Ancient people used bows in what is now Europe, Asia, Africa, and the Americas.

Archery was used for hunting and warfare. People in ancient China used crossbows, which later spread to Europe. Crossbows required less strength and skill than traditional bows. Compound bows were invented in the 1960s. Since then, they have become popular with bowhunters. Today, archers hunt in countries around the world. In the United States, the most popular animals to bowhunt include deer, black bears, and elk.

Elk are popular targets for experienced bowhunters. These large animals can weigh hundreds of pounds. They are prized for their huge antlers.

CHAPTER TWO

Bowhunting Gear

Bowhunters can use traditional bows, compound bows, or crossbows. Traditional bows have one bowstring. The archer puts an arrow on the bowstring. As she draws the bowstring, the limbs of the bow store energy. When she lets go of the bowstring, the energy goes to the arrow and makes it shoot.

Arrows shot from traditional bows travel more slowly. But archers using traditional bows can load and shoot arrows quickly. Some hunters feel proud to use simple yet well-made tools.

Compound bows shoot arrows faster than traditional bows. They have special wheels called cams, which store extra power. Compound bows can be hard for bowhunters to draw at first. But the cams help a bowhunter hold the string back while aiming.

Crossbows are easier to load and aim than compound bows. Crossbows have a stock, which is a long part similar to a gun. The bow attaches to the stock. The crossbow holds the bowstring as the archer loads an arrow.

Traditional bows may be easy to load and handle. But hunters must be strong enough to pull back the bowstring and hold it in place.

Many compound bows can be customized. Hunters can purchase different accessories for their bows, such as arrow rests, sights, and stabilizers.

Crossbow arrows can travel as fast as compound arrows. But loading a crossbow takes longer. The string must be drawn back. Then the archer locks the string before adding the arrow.

Bowhunters can choose from several types of arrows. Some arrows are wooden. Aluminum arrows and carbon fiber arrows are lighter. Heavier arrows can hit an animal with greater force.

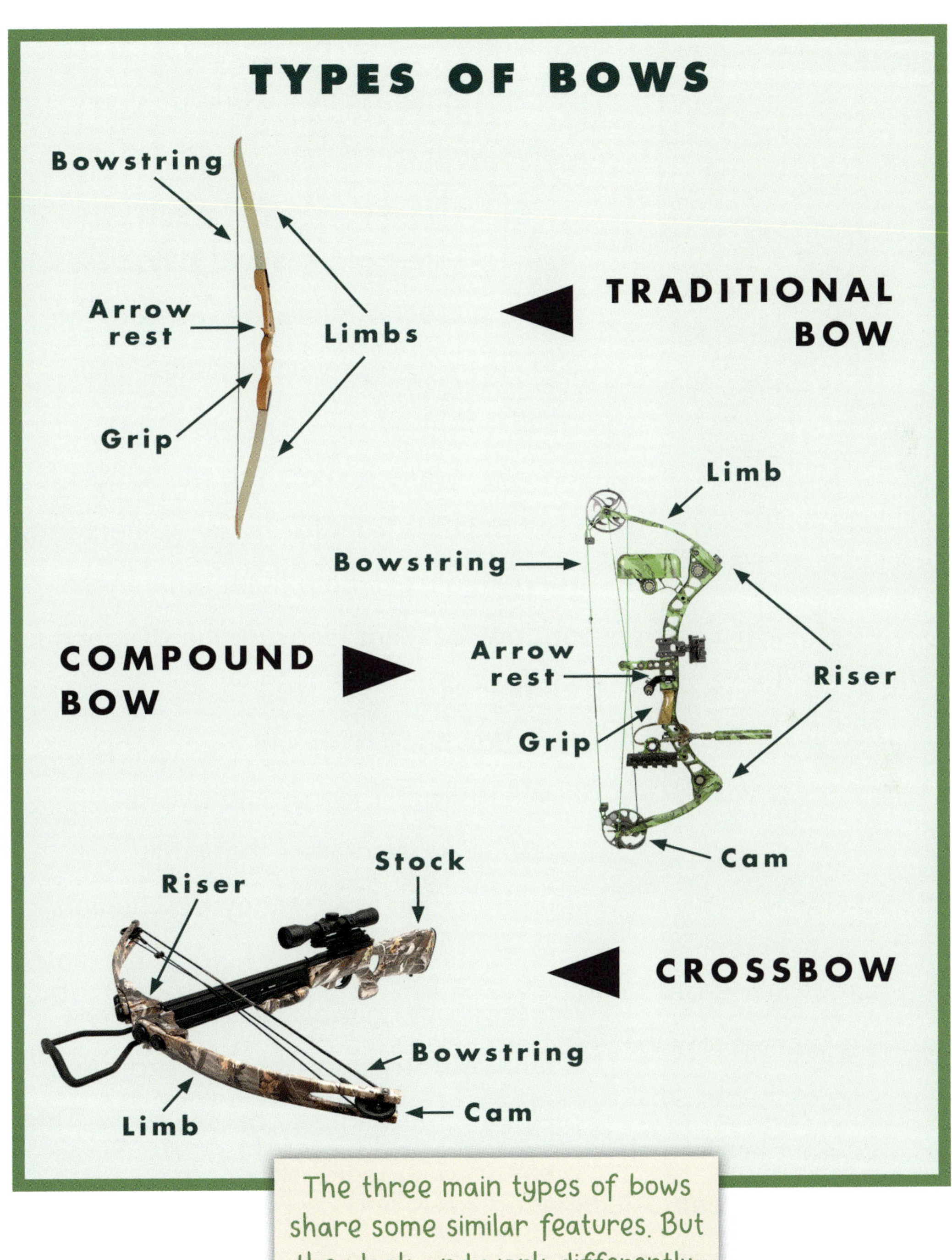

The three main types of bows share some similar features. But they look and work differently.

They are best for big **game** such as bison. Lighter arrows work for small game such as rabbits.

Bowhunters also carry other gear, such as safety glasses and sunglasses. These protect a hunter's eyes from the sun. They also prevent a hunter from getting injured by his bowstring or arrows. Some hunters use binoculars to spot animals from far away. Others use rangefinders to help them aim. These are devices that measure the distance to an animal.

Bowhunters should wear proper clothing, too. They should avoid wearing loose clothes that could get caught by the bow. Many bowhunters wear camouflage. This helps them stay hidden from animals. But bowhunters often wear patches of bright orange or pink so other hunters can see them. This prevents accidental shootings.

BOWFISHING

Some hunters use bows to catch fish. They shoot an arrow connected to a fishing line into the water. The hunter uses the line to pull in fish. Some bowhunters use bowfishing bows. These are lighter and faster than bows used for bigger game. But many hunters use a kit to turn regular bows into bowfishing bows.

Modern rangefinders use laser technology to digitally measure the distance between a bowhunter and his target. This helps improve the accuracy of a hunter's shots.

CHAPTER THREE

ON THE HUNT

Bowhunters must get closer to animals than hunters using guns. With guns, hunters can shoot from up to 1,200 feet (366 m) away. But bowhunters usually need to be closer than 240 feet (73 m). This means bowhunters must understand how animals live and move. Many hunters enjoy this extra challenge.

Some bowhunters stalk their **quarry**. They must move quietly and pay attention to their surroundings. They must also keep track of the wind's direction. Wind can carry a hunter's scent to animals and scare them away.

Other bowhunters wait for their quarry. Some sit in tree stands, or platforms attached to trees. Others wait in blinds. Usually, bowhunters set up tree stands or blinds weeks before a hunt. The stand or blind should be well-hidden and easy for hunters to access. Sometimes hunters sit or stalk for hours and days.

Some bowhunters try to lure game. They buy scents that attract animals. For example, the smell of a doe can attract a buck.

Bowhunters must get close to their targets, so it is important to stay quiet and hidden. In winter, many bowhunters wear snow camouflage to blend in with the environment.

Hunting from a tree stand can help a hunter hide his scent from animals. It also gives the hunter more options for shooting positions and angles.

Other hunters lure game with food or use devices to copy animal calls.

When a bowhunter shoots an animal, it may not die immediately. It may run away. If this happens, the hunter must locate the animal by following clues such as tracks or blood trails. This may take time. But hunters should never abandon killed or hurt animals. They are responsible for the animals they shoot.

After a kill, hunters might field dress the animal. They remove the organs from its body. This keeps the body cool and keeps the meat fresh. Many bowhunters hunt animals for their meat. Even small game like rabbits can make a tasty meal.

Other people hunt to get trophies. Trophies are animals or animal parts that hunters display in their homes. They show off a hunter's success and remind her of past hunts. Deer antlers are one popular trophy. **Taxidermists** can also make a hunted animal's skin into a model.

ANIMAL SCENTS

Many wild animals use their sense of smell to find food, prey, and mates. Using scents can help bowhunters lure an animal close enough to shoot. Many animals approach the smell of food. Others follow a scent when they are curious. Hunters can buy scents at outdoor sports stores. They may come in the form of liquids or sprays. Hunters can dip wicks or strips of fabric in the scent and hang them from nearby branches. Or they can spread a scent around with a spray.

CHAPTER FOUR

GETTING STARTED

Beginners can take classes or archery lessons to learn more about bowhunting. They should also take a hunter education course. This teaches beginners about safety and **sportsmanship**. Hunter education courses may be required to get a hunting license. This gives a person permission to hunt.

To practice good sportsmanship, hunters should learn how to aim accurately. They should try to make clean kills. If a hunter only hurts an animal, or if it takes a long time for a shot to kill the animal, the animal suffers more.

For big game, bowhunters usually aim for the front half of the chest. This holds the heart, lungs, and major blood vessels. A shot in this area causes lots of blood loss, killing the animal faster.

Hunters should also know how to handle their bows safely. They should wear safety glasses and be strong enough to draw and shoot. It can help to practice aiming at a nonliving target. Hunters should never point their weapons at anything other than their targets.

Beginners must take a bowhunting education course, which covers hunting methods and safety. People can also take archery lessons to practice their aim.

Some bowhunters use targets shaped like deer or other commonly hunted animals.

Hunters should know how far they can shoot, too. They should never try shooting anything that is too far away. If a hunter shoots when he is not confident about hitting the target, he might miss or cause animals more suffering.

A beginner should hunt with an experienced adult. She should study how her game behaves and moves. She should also be aware of hunting laws in her area. She should know when the hunting season is for different types of game. Hunting season is the time of year when specific animals can be hunted.

A hunter should also know the bag limit, or how many animals he or she can take. Bag limits help keep animal populations stable.

For example, if hunters kill too many deer, there won't be enough left to breed. The population could fall.

Hunters purchase hunting licenses from state governments. This money is used to fund **conservation**. Conservationists protect land where game animals live. Hunters may directly support conservation efforts, too. By hunting animals, they help control animal populations. This is important because if there are too many deer, for instance, they could eat too many plants and crops. Responsible bowhunters respect the law and the animals they hunt. They help make sure everyone can enjoy the sport of bowhunting.

Experienced bowhunters can pass on their hunting knowledge to beginners. They can teach them how to be safe and responsible while using a bow.

GLOSSARY

archery (AR-chur-ee) Archery is the sport of shooting bows and arrows. Bowhunters practice archery to improve their hunting skills.

compound (KOM-pound) Something that is compound is made out of two or more parts. Arrows shot from compound bows fly faster than arrows shot from traditional bows.

conservation (kon-sur-VAY-shuhn) Conservation is the protection of wildlife and other natural resources. Conservation helps maintain the population of game animals.

game (GAME) Wild animals hunted for food or sport are called game. Many bowhunters target game animals such as bear and deer.

quarry (KWOR-ee) Quarry refers to an animal being hunted. Bowhunters may stalk or lure their quarry.

sportsmanship (SPORTS-muhn-ship) Sportsmanship means acting in a fair and reasonable way. Bowhunters should practice good sportsmanship while on the hunt.

taxidermists (TAK-sih-derm-ists) Taxidermists are people who prepare and mount animal skins to make realistic models of animals. Bowhunters can take the skin or heads of their kills to taxidermists.

traditional (truh-DIH-shuh-nuhl) Something that is traditional is long established or has been practiced for a long time. People have used traditional bows for tens of thousands of years.

FAST FACTS

- In the United States, popular game animals for bowhunting include deer, bear, and elk.
- Bowhunters can pick from three main types of bows: traditional bows, compound bows, and crossbows.
- Bowhunters must get closer to animals than hunters using guns. This means bowhunters must spend more time learning about and watching their quarry.
- Many bowhunters hunt from tree stands or ground blinds. They might try to lure game by using scents or making animal calls.
- Responsible bowhunters respect the law and the animals they hunt.
- Money from hunting licenses goes toward conservation efforts. This involves protecting and improving areas where game animals live.

ONE STRIDE FURTHER

- Why do you think it is important for bowhunters to show good sportsmanship?
- Compare and contrast the three main kinds of bows. Which type of bow would you choose to hunt with and why?
- Some people prefer to hunt with bows. Others like guns. Which would you pick and why?

FIND OUT MORE

IN THE LIBRARY

Bell, Samantha S. *Deer Hunting*. Parker, CO: The Child's World, 2024.

Hemstock, Annie Wendt. *Bow Hunting*. New York, NY: PowerKids Press, 2015.

Nayeri, Daniel. *The Most Dangerous Book: An Illustrated Introduction to Archery*. New York, NY: Workman Publishing, 2017.

ON THE WEB

Visit our website for links about bowhunting:
childsworld.com/links

Note to Parents, Caregivers, Teachers, and Librarians: We routinely verify our Web links to make sure they are safe and active sites. So encourage your readers to check them out!

INDEX